SOMETHING YOU DID

Willy Holtzman

BROADWAY PLAY PUBLISHING INC
224 E 62nd St, NY, NY 10065
www.broadwayplaypub.com
info@broadwayplaypub.com

SOMETHING YOU DID
© Copyright 2008 by Willy Holtzman

First printing: August 2008
I S B N: 0-88145-398-6

Book design: Marie Donovan
Word processing: Microsoft Word
Typographic controls: Ventura Publisher
Typeface: Palatino
Printed and bound in the U S A

SOMETHING YOU DID was originally commissioned by Center Stage (Irene Lewis, Artistic Director) in Baltimore.

SOMETHING YOU DID premiered at People's Light and Theater Company in Malvern PA, running from 18 October to 19 November. The cast and creative contributors were:

UNEEQ . . . . Melanye Finister
ALISON . . . . Amy Van Nostrand
ARTHUR . . . . Jordan Charney
GENE . . . . Tony Campisi
LENORA . . . . Cathy Simpson

Director . . . . Abigail Adams
Set design . . . . James Krozner
Costume design . . . . Marla J Jurglanis
Lighting design . . . . Dennis Parichy
Original music & sound design . . . . Michael Keck
Production stage manager . . . . Kate McSorley

SOMETHING YOU DID opened in New York on
1 April 2008, produced by Primary Stages in association
with Nancy Cooperstein and Betty Ann Besch Solinger.
The cast and creative contributors were:

UNEEQ .... Portia
ALISON .... Joanna Gleason
ARTHUR .... Jordan Charney
GENE .... Victor Slezak
LENORA .... Adriane Lenox

Director .... Carolyn Cantor
Set design .... Eugene Lee
Costume design .... Jenny Mannis
Lighting design .... Jeff Croiter
Original music & sound design .... Lindsay Jones
Production stage manager .... Samone B Weissman
Production supervisor .... P R F Productions
Casting .... Stephanie Klapper Casting

Scene One

(The present. The prison library at a Women's Correctional Facility. ALISON *[white, fifties] wears prison green and shelves books. A guard,* UNEEQ *[black, thirties), sits at a work table and reads from a written statement.)*

UNEEQ: "If I have done anything to hurt anyone, I'm sorry for that."

ALISON: Good. Keep going.

UNEEQ: "But the reasons for the thing I have done can never be known by anyone who isn't me."

ALISON: This is what you want to say?

UNEEQ: I worked very hard on that. I mean, I'm still working...shit, why not?

ALISON: For one thing, it doesn't sound like an admission of guilt.

UNEEQ: What do you mean guilt?

ALISON: Wrongdoing and accountability.

UNEEQ: I know....

ALISON: *Crime and Punishment.*

UNEEQ: I know what guilt is, okay?

ALISON: An offense. An offense that harms other people. With legal consequences and an expectation of restitution. So an admission of guilt is like saying...

UNEEQ: I fucked up. I said that. Okay, so being guilty...

ALISON: ...is ultimately not about how you are seen in the world, but how you see yourself. Are you O K with that?

UNEEQ: I ran a fuckin" stop sign! *(Beat)* It's the "if", isn't it? "If I have done anything..."

ALISON: It undercuts the premise. Conditional, you know. A Catholic in the confessional doesn't say, "If I have sinned, bless me." He says...

UNEEQ: "Bless me, Father, for I have sinned." I'm not stupid, you know.

ALISON: I know.

UNEEQ: Then don't talk to me like I'm stupid.

ALISON: I'm sorry..."if" I gave that impression.

UNEEQ: You are one smart-assed white lady. I might not be "educated," but I learned some things. Things you don't learn in a classroom. You and your "if". "If" my uncle had tits he'd be my aunt.

ALISON: You don't want me to look over the rest of your statement?

UNEEQ: I'll cut the "if"! But don't give me all this attitude doing it. You know, you remind me of my pastor.

ALISON: I doubt that.

UNEEQ: Last Sunday he was going on and on about Lazarus. That's not in the Hebrew bible. You know Lazarus?

ALISON: More or less.

UNEEQ: Then you know how Jesus raised him up from the dead and gave him a second chance at life. That was the theme of the sermon—second chances. To which I say bull-shit.

ALISON: Look, as far as the statement goes, why don't I just mark up the spelling and grammar. Past that, tell the truth.

UNEEQ: Well, there's no lie like the truth. So, we gonna do this thing?

(UNEEQ *hands the statement back to* ALISON. *A buzzer sounds over the door.* ARTHUR, *seventies, enters carrying a briefcase.*)

ARTHUR: I hate prisons. They're always so inconveniently located.

ALISON: This is your way of saying...

ARTHUR: I'm late?

ALISON: A little, Arthur.

ARTHUR: You're busy.

ALISON: We were talking over a legal problem. Uneeq is wondering about her chances for a favorable ruling.

ARTHUR: What are you in for?

UNEEQ: I'm a corrections officer.

ALISON: That's Arthur's idea of a joke.

UNEEQ: I ran a stop sign and they want to charge me two hundred bucks. Can you fix it?

ALISON: Arthur is a legendary fixer among lawyers.

ARTHUR: I don't fix traffic tickets.

UNEEQ: Some lawyer.

ARTHUR: Get me the name of the judge. I'll see what I can do. Might I have some time with my client, Officer...?

UNEEQ: Edmunds. Uneeq Edmunds.

(*Exits*)

ARTHUR: Well, she's aptly named.

ALISON: U-N-E-E-Q.

ARTHUR: Unique spelling.

ALISON: That's not what you're thinking.

ARTHUR: Probably not. You know, the tyranny of political correctness, if I might be so incorrect as to call it that, is the urge to sanitize, no no, to deny, our lower instincts.

ALISON: And that's a bad thing?

ARTHUR: It's an inhuman thing. So forgive me if I think that woman has a ridiculous name she can't even spell correctly.

ALISON: That woman's net pay after taxes is maybe twenty-four thousand. And the piece of crap car she shares with her sister the heroin addict needs a new battery, which she can't afford. So by the time she gets a jump start she's running late for work, and maybe she doesn't make a complete stop at a four-way, okay, rolls...runs the fucking stop sign. No harm, no foul. Any cop would see her Corrections badge and turn a blind eye, professional courtesy. But she's black and she's a woman. So now she has to answer a summons, and maybe pay two hundred dollars from the money she already lacks for a battery, which her sister would probably sell for a fix, anyway.

ARTHUR: Alright, I admit it—I have racist thoughts, I have sexist thoughts. I have, even at my advanced age, thoughts that would make the Marquis de Sade blush. But they're my thoughts and, along with the rare noble thought, that's what makes me human.

ALISON: Forgive me if I keep wanting humans to be humane.

ARTHUR: This Institution is precisely on the way to nowhere. The parkway was down to one lane. Somebody hit a deer. Why there are still deer I don't know. What next, buffalo? Anyway, buckets of blood. And the local traffic, forget about it. Security hasn't gotten any faster here. And for what? So you can bust my chops—is that the phrase?

ALISON: I'm an ingrate, Arthur. I'm not having my best day.

ARTHUR: What would that be, you best day?

ALISON: Any day when I could still do somebody some good.

ARTHUR: Look at all the good you're doing here —AIDS counseling, a literacy program. You're helping Uneeq.

ALISON: A statement to the traffic court. I probably gave her the wrong advice.

ARTHUR: You want me to take her on pro bono?

ALISON: I would never ask.

ARTHUR: Consider it done. You always were a snob. Compassionate, but a snob. Like your father.

ALISON: So we're done talking around that?

ARTHUR: You missed a helluva funeral.

ALISON: Did Lawrence read my tribute?

ARTHUR: Your brother's a fine surgeon, but he was never the speaker you were. Bill Clinton spoke before him. At length. Yes, Lawrence read it. The Trotsky quote got polite applause.
   The warden told me you could have come.

ALISON: In shackles? That would never do, stealing Howard's thunder at his final summation.

ARTHUR: Howard loved you the best. You were his
Gerber red diaper baby. He didn't love you any less
for becoming notorious. It just got complicated.

ALISON: Is complicated love still love?

ARTHUR: You always overanalyzed things.

ALISON: Not everything.

ARTHUR: There was music.

ALISON: Pete Seeger?

ARTHUR: He and Howard went all the way back.
Peekskill, the Black List. As I recall, he taught you
to play guitar. A very sincere man.

ALISON: Terminally sincere. I suppose he sang *This Land
is Your Land.*

ARTHUR: All seventy-five verses.

ALISON: At my funeral I want Dylan.

ARTHUR: *Subterranean Homesick Blues*?

ALISON: Aren't you full of surprises?

ARTHUR: You don't need a weatherman.... We're not
burying you just yet. A number of your old friends
were there.

ALISON: Friends?

ARTHUR: You know, assorted felons and mad bombers
masquerading as University Professors and pundits.
The underground above ground, thickening and
thinning.

ALISON: They haven't aged well?

ARTHUR: Well, they've aged. And they're obviously
shocked by it. Relaxed Fit slacks, tinted hair, frizzy
comb-overs. The A A R P branch of the Howard
Moulton fan club.

ALISON: God knows he kept enough of them out of jail.

ARTHUR: We always had the better lawyers. Those Harvard and Yale preppies couldn't conceive of some C C N Y Jewboys kicking their pampered asses. But we did. Routinely. Better lawyers, better causes.

ALISON: I thought you were the apolitical half of the operation.

ARTHUR: My politics is winning. *(Beat)* Did I mention Gene was there?

ALISON: Gene? Putting pennies on the eyes of the corpse, was he?

ARTHUR: He seemed, I don't know, choked up.

ALISON: That's an old trick of his. That little lump in the throat. He swallows compassion like an anaconda digesting a large rat. You can actually watch it go down.

ARTHUR: That's rather harsh, don't you think?

ALISON: Have you seen his columns, his sanctimonious television tantrums? He's a turncoat and he sold all our secrets to the highest bidder. I hope you told him to go haunt some other cemetery.

ARTHUR: You want me to behave discourteously at a funeral?

ALISON: Did Gene have the courtesy to stay away? To apologize for the sick joke he made of our work? Yes, rude as hell would have been minimally acceptable behavior, especially at your partner's funeral...

ARTHUR: *(Overlapping)* ...your father's...

ALISON: My father's funeral! *(Beat)* It's still not real to me. I keep thinking I'll call and he'll drop names from last night's dinner party, ask me if I'm eating my vegetables.

ARTHUR: Are you?

ALISON: No.

ARTHUR: Me neither.

ALISON: We talked quite often by phone, you know.
It wasn't easy. There's no privacy.

ARTHUR: Howard was always more of a public person.

ALISON: There were things I kept meaning to say. But
he seemed so confused, lately.

ARTHUR: It was the medication. Or the condition. Past
a point, one's as bad as the other. The doctors say he
went peacefully.

ALISON: I wonder what that means?

ARTHUR: It means his suffering was not apparent. He
made us the gift of a good death.

ALISON: I said some words here. In private.

ARTHUR: A prayer?

ALISON: Now, really.

ARTHUR: People get religion. People change. Gene,
for instance.

ALISON: That's twice you brought up his name.

ARTHUR: Is it? That's probably because I spoke to him.

ALISON: You're fucking kidding me.

ARTHUR: You can't expect me to maintain your feuds
for you. There are too many to keep track of at my age.

ALISON: Save the "age" bit for the judges. You didn't
bump into him at all.

ARTHUR: He sought me out. And I welcomed him.
To help you.

ALISON: I can do fine without Gene's help.

ARTHUR: No you cannot! Your pride is astounding, really. I know you come by it honestly, genetically. But Howard exhausted every legal trick in his extensive book of legal tricks.

ALISON: Arthur, there's another parole review coming up.

ARTHUR: And it will go as badly as the last one.

ALISON: Howard never let me make my case. I wrote a statement to the Parole Board and he tore it up.

ARTHUR: He had powerful letters supporting your release. On his death bed was still soliciting letters. Madeleine Albright called to pay her respects, Nelson Mandela. And what did Howard say to them? "Could you write a little something for Alison's file?"

ALISON: It made him feel important.

ARTHUR: Nothing was more important than to see you out of here. He didn't put half as much effort into getting Mandela out.

ALISON: That was different.

ARTHUR: The difference was Nelson Mandela did not commit murder.

ALISON: That's what you think I did?

ARTHUR: What I think doesn't matter. In the eyes of the state you contributed to the death of another human being.

ALISON: There are dozens of women in here for murder. And they'll all get out before I will.

ARTHUR: Because they did it for what? Drugs? Money? Revenge? You did it for politics, excuse me, "revolution". The governor has personally selected your board—a fundamentalist preacher, an ex-cop. The

P B A is crucial to his re-election. And these born-again McCarthy's will never stop making you pay.

ALISON: You think you can make them stop?

ARTHUR: If you let me. But we both know that Howard's way was getting you nowhere. Saint Alison of the Left did not play in Peoria. Sanctimony is for white shoe lawyers. I'm from Brooklyn—I'm a street fighter. We do this my way.

ALISON: Not if your way is Gene.

ARTHUR: Whatever else you think of the guy, he's connected. And his connections go all the way to the Oval Office. Be practical, for once. Don't tie my hands, Alison.

ALISON: I love you, Arthur. But I refuse to let you shake hands with the devil in my name. Don't ever talk to Gene again about me. I forbid it.

ARTHUR: There, just then, that's Howard's voice. High-minded, self-important, self-sabotaging. That's why he had me for a partner. To get things done. Look at me—I can get this done. Let me.

ALISON: You've got a smudge on your glasses.

(ARTHUR *cleans the wrong lens*)

No, there. I caught my reflection in the lenses. It's a game I used to play with Howard when I was a kid. "I can see myself in your glasses. I can see myself in your eyes!" The day he died, I woke up and thought *I've been a reflection all these years.* Well, that's over. I'm not Daddy's little felon anymore. I see what I have to do.

ARTHUR: Are you firing me?

ALISON: That would be crazy. No. I'm arranging a meeting with her.

ARTHUR: Her?

ALISON: Officer Renshaw's daughter.

ARTHUR: Now *that's crazy!* We're not talking a traffic ticket here.

ALISON: I know perfectly well what's at stake.

ARTHUR: I've handled hundreds of paroles. You have to know how to play the game. How to tell your story.

ALISON: Now you want to muzzle me, too? I've already written her.

ARTHUR: If you're trying to send a message to your father, it's a little late.

ALISON: Do me a favor and don't psychoanalyze me. If I make mistakes they'll be my mistakes.

ARTHUR: You'll only make it worse.

ALISON: What could be worse? A man died thirty years ago. And my father died without so much as a daughter at his graveside or a grandchild to carry his name.

ARTHUR: Killing yourself with incarceration will not set the ledger straight.

(A loud bell rings.)

ALISON: That's lunch. There's a turkey sandwich still in the hall vending machine. Or maybe it's roast beef. We could split it.

ARTHUR: Got to run—traffic. I almost forgot. This was on the nightstand next to Howard's bed. *(He removes an old cardigan from his briefcase and hands it to ALISON)* I thought you might want it.

ALISON: Doesn't exactly go with prison greens.

ARTHUR: I can drop it in the Goodwill bin.

ALISON: It does get chilly here. Someone will use it.

ARTHUR: Just to be on the safe side. *(Sets the sweater on the library cart)*

ALISON: I never told him I was sorry.

ARTHUR: He knew. He never stopped loving you. *(Exits)*

(ALISON walks towards sweater on the library cart then turns away.)

Scene Two

(The consulting office of GENE BIDDLE. GENE *cradles a phone against his shoulder.* ARTHUR *enters and stands.)*

GENE: ...we would be crazy to take less than seven figures as an advance... *(Gestures for* ARTHUR *to sit)* But it *will* be a best seller, the Foundation guarantees that...So the *Times* puts a little dagger thing next to it on the list, who gives a shit? ...But Ben...Ben...*Ben*, I'm going to put you on the speaker phone...It's not a cheap power play. I've got a crick in my neck... Okay?

BEN: *(Voice on speaker phone)* I know a good chiropractor.

GENE: I'll send you the bill. The bottom line is...

BEN: *(Voice)* Did you actually say "bottom line?"

GENE: Grow up, Ben. The point is I will not sign to write the book for less than a million up front.

BEN: *(Voice)* I published your first book. Abbie Hoffman was already on the shelf with *Steal This Book*. But they stole yours.

GENE: I'm making up for lost time. And royalties. Best to Martha. *(Hangs up. He crosses to* ARTHUR *and shakes his hand)* Arthur Rossiter in my office. I'm honored. Please, sit.

ARTHUR: That was a cheap power play.

GENE: Yes. But it worked.

ARTHUR: Ben Clarkson?

GENE: Friend of yours?

ARTHUR: Client. This is going back years. I helped him clear up a little accounting unpleasantness with Simon and Schuster.

GENE: Ben is a significant shareholder.

ARTHUR: It worked out pleasantly for him in the end. Hell of an advance you're demanding.

GENE: I'll settle for three quarters of it.

ARTHUR: Still real money. But I guess if the subject matter sells...

GENE: You bet it sells.

ARTHUR: Might I know the subject?

GENE: You might, in which case you might tell me.

ARTHUR: You're bargaining like that when you don't even know what you're going to write?

GENE: Something always comes up. Maybe I should write about you.

ARTHUR: Oh, that'll sell like hotcakes.

GENE: You never know—successful lawyer with crypto-Commie connections. Besides, it's my name they sell anyway.

ARTHUR: I might own that, once I get done suing you.

GENE: Okay, tough guy, put your guns back in the holster. I was just having some fun with you. How do you like the office?

ARTHUR: *(Looks around)* This is very...grown up. You're obviously doing well for yourself.

GENE: All rented—it's nothing.

ARTHUR: A book advance of "seven figures" is not nothing.

GENE: Take away performance bonuses, commissions, tax, it's not so much as all that.

ARTHUR: And this foundation you were talking about?

GENE: The book will sell on its own. I have a loyal, literate readership and they're not shy about buying books.

ARTHUR: But if they don't, in sufficient numbers to put you on the Times list? The what Foundation fills in.

GENE: Allard. The Allard Foundation.

ARTHUR: Didn't they sponsor a series of cross burnings?

GENE: Do you want an answer to your question, or do you want to take liberal potshots? The Allard Foundation is prepared to make bulk purchases and distribute them at conventions and fundraisers. Instant bestseller.

ARTHUR: With a dagger.

GENE: Okay, it's not strictly individual retail purchases. So what? The way books are hustled and whored these days, they all should have daggers—O'Reilly, Coulter, Hillary.

ARTHUR: If Hillary had a real dagger...

GENE: She'd cut my balls off. Yeah, yeah, yeah. I take it you read my latest column?

ARTHUR: I didn't want to bring up the Hillary bashing. I might have said it's misogynistic, gutter politics and it's been done to death by radio talk thugs who don't have a fraction of your intellect.

GENE: That's what you might have said?

ARTHUR: But I didn't want to be rude.

GENE: You invented rude.

ARTHUR: If I might be uncharacteristically polite—congratulations. This is some operation you've created. Books, on-line opinion columns, magazine pieces, speeches, political consulting, foundations. You're omnipresent. The first time you came into the office, hair down to here, jeans hanging by a thread, a nobody wanting legal advice for what? I'm trying to remember...

GENE: Inciting to riot.

ARTHUR: You threw something. A brick.

GENE: A paving stone. Sounds more classically revolutionary that way.

ARTHUR: Ah, poor Bank of America. So much inviting plate glass.

GENE: They were underwriting a half-dozen brutal dictatorships.

ARTHUR: We pled you down to unlawful assembly.

GENE: Your memory is better than you think.

ARTHUR: You stood in front of Howard and me and lectured us about how the judicial system was the corrupt oppressive arm of an illegitimate fascist regime.

GENE: Your memory gets better and better.

ARTHUR: You said you were going to turn that courtroom into a circus. You even rented a clown suit. And I told you...

GENE: To "shut the fuck up". You wanted to put it in terms I would understand.

ARTHUR: You understood the term "pro bono" well enough.

GENE: What do you want? I was broke.

ARTHUR: And now you're grown up.

GENE: Arthur, if I didn't know better I'd say you're giving me shit.

ARTHUR: That you would even suggest such a thing.

GENE: Now you're giving me shit about giving me shit. You have a hell of a way of reminiscing.

ARTHUR: You put an old friend in the ground, where else are your thoughts going to go but backwards?

GENE: I didn't know you and Howard were friends, exactly.

ARTHUR: I meant you. He was your friend, no? In any case, it was very gracious of you to attend.

GENE: A man is known by his friends.

ARTHUR: And enemies. Were you expecting to run into a certain old friend turned mortal enemy?

GENE: I'm not going to talk about Alison.

ARTHUR: You'll admit it would have been a notable encounter.

GENE: You know, getting you to the fucking point... it's still three dimensional chess, and as far as I can tell you haven't lost anything off your game.

ARTHUR: All those phony radical intellectuals. You were the only one could keep up with me. That's why I came to like you, in spite of yourself.

GENE: And now there's no end of things to dislike about me. Have I become "impure"? Whored myself?

ARTHUR: Depends who's writing the checks.

GENE: Who's writing your checks, Arthur?

ARTHUR: You know, Howard mostly saved the virtuous cases for himself. The ones that got him A-list invitations, awards, testimonials. A half page *Times* obituary above the fold!

GENE: And you got?

ARTHUR: Drug dealers, delinquent landlords, corporate miscreants, ambulances to chase. I got to pay the bills for Moulton and Rossiter.

GENE: I'm just paying some bills here.

ARTHUR: Does that include moral debts? I mean, I have to say I was surprised to see you at the funeral, considering the colossal right turn you made in your politics.

GENE: It did have a certain shock value.

ARTHUR: It was nothing less than electrifying. Joan Baez actually walked to the other side of the grave.

GENE: Oh, like she's the conscience of the nation because she sang *Joe Hill* at Woodstock?

ARTHUR: Why did you come up to me at the funeral?

GENE: I came to pay my respects to your partner.

ARTHUR: Bullshit. You came to me to see if partners share files. To see if certain secrets were buried with the corpse.

GENE: Secrets, conspiracies. The great bugaboo of the Left.

ARTHUR: This is some highway you drive, my friend. Right side, left side, don't cross the center line. What could be simpler?

GENE: Spare me the self-righteous bit. I've heard it before.

ARTHUR: Alison Moulton is sitting in a prison cell going on thirty years. That's wrong.

GENE: And a New York City cop is rotting in a grave, only he's never coming out. Tell me what that is?

ARTHUR: Also wrong.

GENE: You can read about it in my next column.

ARTHUR: Blocking Alison's parole is not going to bring that man back to life.

GENE: Letting her out would kill justice. It would insult every cop who ever gave his life in the line of duty.

ARTHUR: You called cops "pigs". In open court.

GENE: That was harmless rhetoric.

ARTHUR: You don't see a little inconsistency here?

GENE: Oh, come out and say it.

ARTHUR: Hypocrisy! You were a spoiled little post doc with smooth hands and contempt for real working men. Now you're a man of the people.

GENE: You just can't stand that I speak for the folks.

ARTHUR: Yeah, rich folks. I can name at least six corporations that fund the Allard Foundation with lawsuits pending on environmental abuse, worker safety, product safety, people drinking rancid groundwater, dying in leukemia clusters-folks, Gene. The ones you champion, when it's convenient. Like it was convenient in the sixties.

GENE: You know, I get so sick of people telling me about the change in my politics. You want to know about change? Go down to Ground Zero. Take a look at the hole where there used to be shining towers. Take a good look around the neighborhood—they're still finding bone fragments! Then take a look at the kids coming out of Walter Reed with titanium rods where there used to be arms and legs. And tell me a bomb is just a symbol. Tell me terror is a legitimate tool for change. I didn't change. The world changed. If you want to insult me, be my guest. But do not insult my intelligence. And don't even think of asking me to support Alison's parole appeal as some sort of dirty little quid pro quo. Because I would sooner die.

ARTHUR: You've got all this media at your beck and call. So you use a little of it for a good cause.

GENE: She's a cop killer. She was there when the bomb went off!

ARTHUR: I see, there's guilt in proximity. What precisely was your proximal guilt, Gene? Before you answer, you should know there are other records.

GENE: There is nothing in the public record on me.

ARTHUR: Private records that could be made public. Howard and I might have fought. There were times we couldn't stand the sight of each other, right to the bitter end. But we were partners. We shared files. I know your secrets.

GENE: This is a clear breach of the attorney-client privilege.

ARTHUR: This is advocacy. Documents show up in dumpsters, on email.

GENE: You're bluffing. I'll have you brought up on charges.

ARTHUR: You'll never lay a hand on me. I only want you to do what's right. See her. Is that asking so much?

GENE: Don't lawyer me, Arthur. You can't force me to advocate her release, and you know it.

ARTHUR: I'm just an old man. What can I do? Starting Monday morning, I clean out Howard's files. I sit at his desk, a trash can on one side, a box for the New York Times on the other. One right, one left. All very simple.

That's what I'll be doing next week. What you'll be doing is your business. *(Exits)*

Scene Three

(The prison library. UNEEQ *stands with a carefully tailored middle-aged black woman,* LENORA.*)*

UNEEQ: I guess she's running late.

LENORA: I make a point of punctuality.

UNEEQ: You do time by the calendar, not by the clock. And prisoners got to be stripped searched before visitation. That's DOCS policy. Things here move at their own speed. Your first time in a maximum security prison?

LENORA: *(Nods)* It is secure? I saw one guard tower with one guard reading a magazine. That strikes me as minimal, to say the least.

UNEEQ: There's a reason for that—women don't try to escape.

LENORA: I find that hard to believe.

UNEEQ: I'm telling you it's for real. I got some thoughts about it.

LENORA: I'm certain you do.

UNEEQ: A man thinks he can run from things. A woman knows wherever you run, there you are. You can't escape from yourself.

LENORA: That's your theory?

UNEEQ: That's my observation.

LENORA: Forgive me if that doesn't make me feel particularly secure.

(The door buzzes, ALISON *rushes in.)*

ALISON: I hope you haven't been waiting long.

LENORA: Eight minutes.

ALISON: I'm so sorry. There was a disturbance in the yard and then it was time for count.

(To UNEEQ*)*

Pearl tried to escape again.

LENORA: *(To* UNEEQ*)* I thought you said...

UNEEQ: Pearl's not a prisoner. She's a Labrador Retriever. *(She positions herself out of earshot on the other side of a locked mesh gate.)*

ALISON: Puppies Behind Bars. We socialize them for Guiding Eyes. Alison Moulton. Of course, you know that.

LENORA: Lenora Renshaw. I want to keep this as brief as possible.

ALISON: Yes, whatever you say. You received my letter?

LENORA: I also received a letter from the Parole Board notifying me of your upcoming hearing and inviting me to make a statement.

ALISON: I haven't decided if I'm going to make a statement to the Board.

LENORA: I'm surprised. It's a new panel. A minister, I'm told. Perhaps more open-minded, more forgiving. *(Beat)* Yellow or black?

ALISON: I'm sorry?

LENORA: The Labrador puppy.

ALISON: Yes. Chocolate. I guess that's the fashion just now.

LENORA: I wouldn't know.

ALISON: We spoil them rotten. The training comes later. First comes love. It's gratifying, knowing my puppy will be somebody's eyes. I close my eyes sometimes and imagine her crossing the street, sitting next to a park bench, watching a squirrel. I envy her.

LENORA: If we might discuss your letter. It is a very well-crafted apology. You say all the right things. But I can't help wondering about the timing. All these years without so much as a word. Why now?

ALISON: I wrote a thousand different letters. But on the advice of counsel...

LENORA: Your father.

ALISON: ...I didn't send one.

LENORA: Now you're keeping your own counsel. I can't tell you how often I've driven past this place.

ALISON: I hear cars go by at night.

LENORA: I went over and over in my mind what I would say to you, given the chance. Today I drove into the prison parking lot and every word went out of my head. I started the car again to go home, but Sam Cooke came on the radio.

ALISON: Sam Cooke?

LENORA: He was on the radio that day at the shoeshine stand. Did you know that?

ALISON: I don't notice music as much as I should.

LENORA: That was always the first thing my father noticed. "You know a person by his music." He loved Sam Cooke. Heard a lot of church in his voice. My father had quite a nice voice.

ALISON: Do you take after him that way?

LENORA: I don't sing. I talk. I talked at eight months. I made the high school debating team as a freshman.

ALISON: I don't want to debate you.

LENORA: No, you do not. *(Removes a medal from her purse)* I won a medal.

ALISON: *(Reads)* "Bronx Science." That's where the really smart kids went.

LENORA: No affirmative action. Strictly merit.

ALISON: Your father must have been very proud.

LENORA: To have a daughter amongst all those Jewish and Chinese chess playing fools? He was proud as hell. Mind you, I'm not in the habit of showing off high school accolades. I just threw it in some drawer. He must have found it. *(Presses the medal into* ALISON's *hand)* He had it on him when he died. Look. The heat of the blast vaporized the anodized coating—that's the discoloration. That and the blood, which has the properties of dye, they tell me.

*(*ALISON *gives the medal back to* LENORA*.)*

LENORA: Senior year I was all-City champion. My teachers encouraged me to go into politics, but I was raised to believe politics is a dirty business. We were church people, not political people.

ALISON: I was raised to think politics is religion.

LENORA: And when exactly did you get "religion"?

ALISON: It's not something you can pinpoint.

LENORA: I bet if you really tried...

ALISON: Where to start? There's the Vietnam War, obviously, but by then I already had "religion". I'm trying to think, was there one leaflet, one headline, one of a countless dinner conversations growing up? *(Beat)* No. My political conversion, if you want to call it that, I guess I'd have to say the Civil Rights Movement.

LENORA: Ah, the Negro cause.

ALISON: I took a Greyhound to McComb, Mississippi. In 1964.

LENORA: Your parents just let you go?

ALISON: My father put me on the bus. By the time I got off, three workers had already gone missing.

LENORA: I know the landscape well. I have relations in Greenwood. I know how the locals look at me whenever I come to visit in my city clothes and cadences. How I look them straight back in the eye. I wonder how they looked at you when you got off that Greyhound?

ALISON: I was threatened, taunted, spat on. And then I went out to register voters even after those workers turned up dead.

LENORA: I'm sure your father was very proud of you. My father barely let me out of the house.

ALISON: But your mother?

LENORA: My mother passed when I was young. My father was mother and father to me. I mean, every morning he put on a uniform and was the only black police officer in a precinct where the only other black man was cleaning toilets. Worked double shifts, weekends directing traffic around construction sites, and fell asleep in front of the television most nights because he was too tired to drag himself to bed. All that to put me through college and keep me off the streets. But you came back from Mississippi and decided the street was political.

ALISON: I was out there protesting injustice.

LENORA: I was in a classroom. I made something of my life. You made bombs.

ALISON: We turned to armed struggle as a last resort. And we targeted property, not people. Every explosion was preceded by a precise warning.

LENORA: Where was my father's warning?

ALISON: That was not planned. Malcolm was only supposed to plant the device.

LENORA: In Grand Central Terminal.

ALISON: In a locker, with a timer, with an evacuation phone call. Your father surprised him.

LENORA: He was walking his beat. Doing his job. You saw the whole thing, didn't you?

ALISON: We worked in pairs. I was positioned at the shoeshine stand.

LENORA: You could have shouted a warning. Run up to Malcolm like he was your brother home for the holidays. My father would have walked away. Lived a full life.

ALISON: I didn't see it coming.

LENORA: I'm trying to come to terms with this. Find some peace at long last. But there are gaps. And the pictures in my head, they might be wrong, they might be worse than what was. It would help me to know what you saw.

ALISON: It happened so fast.

LENORA: I need to know what you saw. You owe me that much. The bomb went off. Then what?

ALISON: *(Beat)* The light is sudden, blinding. I'm gulping air, trying to cough the smoke out of my lungs. I'm aware, aware, of people screaming, running, crawling.

LENORA: Two men. Motionless?

ALISON: Malcolm was unrecognizable as a man.
Blown apart.

LENORA: And my father? Dynamite packs quite a
punch. At close range the heat makes your blood boil.
My father was filled with bubbles, like neglected soup.
But that's not what killed him, is it?

ALISON: When you also have generalized blunt trauma...

LENORA: What?

ALISON: What the doctors call tissue disruption...

LENORA: I'm the daughter of a police officer. Police
officers look after each other's widows and orphans.
Police officers share crucial information that slick
lawyers keep out of the legal record. Tell me what
killed my father.

ALISON: *(With difficulty)* A nail.

LENORA: One nail?

ALISON: He was struck by several.

LENORA: And when does a bomb stop being symbolic?
When does an explosive device become an
anti-personnel weapon?

ALISON: When somebody fills it with nails.

LENORA: Who did the filling?

ALISON: I never made a bomb. Not once.

LENORA: Somebody made those little calling cards your
people left at the Draft Bureau, the Capitol Building.
But none of them had nails.

ALISON: Our military was using cluster bombs...

LENORA: Somebody bought those nails. It's not in
the record because your father cut a deal. Stopped
the proceedings cold rather than risk having that come

out in testimony. This is your testimony. Who bought the nails?

ALISON: We don't inform on each other.

LENORA: Is that supposed to be honorable? Where's the honor in protecting a murderer? That bomb was designed to kill people.

ALISON: It was meant to be a deterrent.

(LENORA *crosses to the upstage door to exit.* ALISON *pursues her.)*

ALISON: We wanted to show what a cluster bomb can do. Malcolm must have somehow crossed the detonator wires.

LENORA: What if he meant to be a suicide bomber?

ALISON: That scenario was never even discussed.

LENORA: But Malcolm didn't make careless errors, did he? He knew exactly what he was doing. I knew a hundred Malcolm's at Bronx Science. A mind like that wouldn't even have to write it down to work the equations. The velocity of shrapnel over a given area. The spray patterns. The likelihood of tissue trauma. The probability of death. He knew all the permutations.

ALISON: I didn't know what was in his head.

LENORA: There was a nail in the back of my father's head. That was the cause of death. It was not instantaneous. A slow bleeder, they said. I can't get that picture out of my mind. I can't stop wondering what was in his mind. Did he see you? Did he see me? Did he see the future? A wedding with no father to give the bride away. No one to call when the marriage breaks up. Grandchildren without a grandfather.

ALISON: I'm not asking your forgiveness. I don't expect you to support my parole.

LENORA: What, then?

ALISON: Don't prevent it.

LENORA: That's asking a great deal. What if you're released? How does that help my father?

ALISON: I can still help other people.

LENORA: The parole report says you're doing that here.

ALISON: More people; help them learn from my mistakes.

LENORA: And you want nothing for yourself?

ALISON: I want to make up for what I did. I want your mercy.

LENORA: You can do better than that.

ALISON: I want to do what people do. Sit on a park bench. Watch a squirrel. Do nothing. I want to be free to live what's left of my life!

LENORA: *(Beat)* I believe you.

ALISON: I don't expect you to answer right away.

LENORA: No. I told myself I would not leave here until I made up my mind one way or the other. It's not as if I need to discuss this with anyone. I'm an only child. And my children, they only want to be quit of the whole thing. Since they never knew their grandfather, it's hard for them to feel the loss. *(Beat)* I understand you just lost your father. My condolences. Was it sudden?

ALISON: A long illness.

LENORA: Then you had a chance to say goodbye to his face. Do they allow that?

ALISON: Under certain circumstances. I chose not to. We spoke on the phone.

LENORA: You told him you were sorry you ended up in this place. You told him you loved him.

ALISON: Whether we say it or not, we love our fathers.

LENORA: What I said to my father...We had an argument. A debate, you might say. Frightfully one-sided. Pathetic, really, with his high school equivalency diploma and me halfway through college. I was home for summer break. He was out the door for work when his shift supervisor called about something. "Can I speak to Soul Brother Number One?" I hand him the phone and he gets that amiable tone going. He gets off and I'm all over him. "How can you let that cracker call you that?" "He's not a cracker. That's just what the guys call me. What's the big deal? That's what people call James Brown." "James Brown has a head full of pomade and votes for Nixon." "How do you know I didn't vote for him?" "Because only an Uncle Tom would vote for Nixon." Mind you, this is championship debating technique. Frustrate your opponent into an opening, then go for the kill. I killed something in my father. I could see it in his face. It was as if I said "I hate you." I could have stopped him at the door, on the porch, in the car. Taken it back. "That came out all wrong. You know I love you, daddy." But I was too proud. I told myself I'll wait for him to come home. I'll apologize later. There was no later. *(Beat)* The officer who came to tell me of my father's death, I barely knew him. Never heard from him again. But I saw his name in the paper a few years ago. He was in the South Tower when it came down. And everything came rushing back up to me.

(Overlapping)

ALISON: I'm so sorry.

LENORA: You, Grand Central, everything.

ALISON: Please tell me...

LENORA: I can't put it out of my mind.

ALISON: ...what do you want from me?

LENORA: What do I want? I want my father back! I want
the chance to be a better daughter. *(Beat)* I'm a merciful
woman. I've tried to lead a good life. A life that would
make my father proud. I came here for him. He would
want me to pat you on the back, "The past is past. No
hard feelings." *(She motions to* UNEEQ.*)* But I'm not him.
I'm not that strong.

ALISON: I'm so sorry.

LENORA: We disappoint our fathers, don't we?

ALISON: I'm sorry for everything.

LENORA: I can't use your sorrow.

*(*LENORA *takes her purse and exits.)*

*(*ALISON *suddenly feels cold. She finds her father's cardigan
and slips it on. She slips her hands in the pockets. From one
pocket she removes a printed sheet of paper folded in fours.
She unfolds it and reads it to herself.)*

Scene Four

(The prison library. ALISON *shelves books.* UNEEQ *checks the
log book.)*

UNEEQ: Worked like a charm. My statement.

ALISON: I give expert advice, to other people.

UNEEQ: I told the judge all about my sister. He was
moved.

ALISON: How could you tell?

UNEEQ: He put down his crossword puzzle, looked
me square in the eye and said, "What did you say your
name was?" He not only threw out the ticket, he asked

if he could "intercede on my behalf". I didn't even
know I had a behalf for anyone to intercede on.
If I knew the truth worked, I would've started using
it a long time ago. *(Beat)* Did it work on that woman
with her tailored suit and Presbyterian attitude?

ALISON: Presbyterian?

UNEEQ: She ain't going to no Baptist church with those
big words and that nose in the air elocution of hers.
Baptists don't need words at all when they're filled
with the Holy Ghost. No speakin" in tongues for Mrs....

ALISON: Ms Renshaw.

UNEEQ: She would be a Ms. new school, I mean.
Old school was how you showed respect to a woman
without calling into question her marital status. More
like "muz". Muz Sanders, Muz Robideau, Muz Brown.
None of this "M" "S" shit. Does she have a first name?

ALISON: Lenora.

UNEEQ: Lenora. Lenora. Nobody has that name.
That's a name for somebody don't know who she is,
or knows and hates it. I guess she hated you, alright.

ALISON: I guess she did.

UNEEQ: You fucked up, and somebody died. But you
not the first person ever fucked up, and if that parole
board keeps you here till you evaporate, it won't make
you the last.

ALISON: I don't know that anyone can change their
minds at this point.

UNEEQ: Don't count out that old lawyer you got coming
here. Hey, you don't think he called my judge, do you?

ALISON: Why do you ask?

UNEEQ: Because I don't much like the man. He smiles.
Not with his mouth. His eyes. You ask yourself, is this

asshole laughing at me? You know what I'm saying?
I don't want him enjoying himself at my expense.
Even if he is kind of a sexy old son of a bitch.

ALISON: Arthur, sexy?

UNEEQ: He looked at my ass like it was on the menu.
And he looked again, for good measure.

ALISON: Wait, you don't trust him?

UNEEQ: A man his age puttin' that kind of shit out
there? I'd trust him with my life!

(*A buzzer sounds. The door opens and* ARTHUR *appears,
not quite entering the library.*)

UNEEQ: Speak of the devil.

ARTHUR: The abuse I take.

ALISON: Uneeq thinks you gave her the once over.

ARTHUR: You think I'm too old to appreciate a woman?

ALISON: This is nothing to do with age. It's about
discretion.

ARTHUR: Well I'm too old to be discreet.

UNEEQ: That's for damned sure.

ARTHUR: Behave yourself. (*To* ALISON) I brought
important company.

(ARTHUR *enters and holds open the door.* GENE *appears.*)

ALISON: No, no. No! I will not do this, Arthur.

(*Overlapping*)

GENE: It's good to see you, too, Al.

UNEEQ: Who is this individual?

ALISON: Whatever you two are up to, I don't want any
part of it.

ARTHUR: Eugene Biddle. Mister Biddle would like some time to consult with Alison about her parole appeal.

ALISON: Consult?

UNEEQ: Are you an attorney?

ALISON: I don't consult with assholes.

GENE: I'm a journalist.

ALISON: He wrote that African-Americans should be grateful for slavery.

UNEEQ: Excuse me?

GENE: What I wrote was despite the methods that brought them to these shores, black people enjoy a better standard of living here than black people anywhere else in the world.

UNEEQ: Is there anything else I should know about him?

ALISON: He broke his mother's heart.

GENE: My mother was a Communist.

ARTHUR: Communists don't have hearts.

ALISON: I don't want him here.

UNEEQ: No inmate can be visited against her will. Come with me.

ARTHUR: Nobody's going anywhere. Except me and Uneeq.

UNEEQ: Oh, you calling the shots?

ARTHUR: I called Judge Rubio.

UNEEQ: All non-attorney visits are supervised.

ARTHUR: As you know, Officer Edmonds, representatives of the news media are permitted to have unsupervised visits at the discretion of the attending C O. It could be highly beneficial to my client.

UNEEQ: I will supervise this visit—from the other side of that door. Unless the prisoner has an objection.

ARTHUR: Alison, please—give him ten minutes. I sat in traffic for two hours with this man. It was like being locked in hell with Dick Cheney.

ALISON: Ten minutes. Not a minute more.

UNEEQ: Ten minutes. *(Exiting with* ARTHUR*)* You did look at my ass, didn't you?

ARTHUR: So sue me.

UNEEQ: I'll do more than that you do more than look.

GENE: *(Long pause)* She's a real ball-buster.

ALISON: Another ungrateful descendent of slaves.

GENE: Nice of you to bring that up, first thing. *(Beat)* You look the same.

ALISON: No I don't.

GENE: You look pretty damn good, all things considered.

ALISON: If you're implying that incarceration agrees with me...

GENE: Compared to some of the lost causes I've run into lately.

ALISON: I assume you're speaking of the people you saw at Howard's funeral. I wonder how they saw you?

GENE: The Anti-Christ in their midst, no doubt. How do I look?

ALISON: Seriously middle-aged.

GENE: Oh, thanks.

ALISON: You always looked middle-aged. Even when you were young. That's why we sent you to the liquor store.

GENE: That and the fact that I paid. Good. So you're saying I haven't changed, I think.

ALISON: Physically. Politically?

GENE: Let's not go there, just yet.

ALISON: I see, it's a switch you turn on and off.

GENE: We're political animals, you and I, even if our politics have moved to opposite sides of the jungle. But I wonder if we might be human with each other before we start showing our fangs.

ALISON: Arthur finds my "humanity" oppressive.

GENE: So we'll make small talk.

ALISON: It's possible I'm a little rusty.

GENE: Prisoners don't make small talk?

ALISON: They crave it. Makes them feel part of the world. Basketball is very big, especially women's basketball.

GENE: Popular with lesbians, I'm told.

ALISON: Sorry to disappoint you, but I don't have any racy women behind bars stories for you. People here tend to come to me for big talk. Maybe they need help with their G E Ds. Maybe their Ex is dying. Maybe they're dying.

GENE: You always were a good listener.

ALISON: Talkers always assume that.

GENE: Talk to me, Al. Jesus, after thirty years we ought to have something to talk about.

ALISON: *(Beat)* How's the family?

GENE: Okay. I'm still married to Phyllis. She's redecorating the house—again. Ellen is in graduate school. Robert is a corporate attorney, married last year. I'm not yet a grandfather. I make a living.

ALISON: Quite a good living.

GENE: Don't believe everything you read in the papers.

ALISON: What do your children think of their father?

GENE: Scourge of the Left, nefarious neo-Con—that sort of thing? They know as well as I do that a neo-Conservative

ALISON: is just a liberal who's been mugged. I figure they're both in their twenties. That's still considered young, isn't it?

GENE: I believe Jerry Rubin set the cut-off age at thirty. The Who was less specific. "Hope I d-die before I get old." We got old—is that the message?

ALISON: No message, right? Just talk. You taught your kids youth is the time for idealism? Rebellion?

GENE: Nobody's that young, anymore.

ALISON: Then the world got old. Graduate school in what?

GENE: Early Renaissance Art. She thinks the world was a terrific place in the fifteenth century. She's a registered Democrat and, depending on her mood, mostly disregards me, not so much for my politics as for the fact that I don't know the difference between Donatello and Michelangelo, and couldn't care less. You don't see me getting upset because she still confuses *The Nation* and *The National Review*. Robert's primary anxiety is that he will turn thirty before he makes his second million.

ALISON: The Biddles are living the bourgeois dream.

GENE: I may have become an outspoken capitalist. That doesn't mean I'm any good at it.

ALISON: Are you happy, Gene?

GENE: Never happier.

ALISON: Give me an honest, direct answer. Do you miss it?

GENE: It?

ALISON: You know, the old times.

GENE: Oh, God no, not that "it"? The *sixties*!

ALISON: When you say it like that...

GENE: You want, what, hushed, reverential tones? I think at this late date even you have to admit it's all gotten a bit Disney. I'm sick to death of the big question. What did you do in the sixties, daddy? The real question is was there ever really a sixties at all?

ALISON: Oh, come on.

GENE: Okay, okay, okay. There are probably moments in the dark of night when I have a kind of twinge, a longing even, for, how shall I put it? the Good Old Days when we knew there would be better days to come. Then I take a Xanax and wait for it all to pass.

ALISON: You were wound a little tight when it came to drugs.

GENE: I focused on the sex, which I recall was abundant and superb.

ALISON: Speak for yourself.

GENE: You can sit there and say it wasn't?

ALISON: With you? I guess alright.

GENE: I'm overwhelmed by your enthusiasm.

ALISON: I think back to the first time we met. And what sticks out most in my mind is your glasses. Black horn-rims. Very Buddy Holly.

GENE: I was going more for Allen Ginsberg. A straight Allen Ginsberg.

GENE: You were, what, leather mini-skirt, boots, bomber jacket?

ALISON: That was somebody else. Peasant blouse, ripped jeans, upside down American flag patch.

GENE: You wore your ideals. Until they wore through.

ALISON: I still have my ideals. You want to pretend the past never existed.

GENE: I don't deny the past. I just consign it to its proper developmental place, like acne.

ALISON: Is there anything you don't mock?

GENE: The "sixties" was a mockery of political discourse.

ALISON: Anything that's not a sound bite?

GENE: We told ourselves we were revolutionaries. We didn't have a clue. We were baby boomer brats who despised authority. Nothing changed. We were miserable for nothing.

ALISON: I have nostalgia for misery. So much suffering in the world, and the Biddles are redecorating. Being miserable for a cause is what I miss.

GENE: I've come to terms with the past.

ALISON: By lying about it?

GENE: By getting on with my life.

ALISON: I am confronted by the past every waking hour. Do I regret it? Yes! Do I miss it? Yes!

GENE: Well, you'll be happy to know the bombing thing caught on like crazy. First kid on your block.

ALISON: That's right, Gene. I practically invented gunpowder.

GENE: Don't be modest. You helped improvise your share of explosive devices. But it was one thing when you were playing political pranks with overgrown firecrackers. When it came to secret cells, soft targets, shrapnel, you crossed a line—you created a template for terror!

ALISON: Don't you dare put that on me.

GENE: Your self-delusion is stunning. You still live in that little leftist dream world.

ALISON: I live here. I have more reality in twenty-four hours here than you've had in your entire life.

GENE: It's merely a different kind of artificiality. You're no more blue-collared or black-skinned than you were back in the day. Your guard friend. Do you actually think she likes you?

ALISON: You think that's impossible because she dislikes you?

GENE: She detested me on sight. That's without reading my books or witnessing my television rants. She detests the idea of me, because I'm a Jew.

ALISON: You're a Quaker.

GENE: A lapsed Quaker. And before that a lapsed Jew from a long line of lapsed Jews.

ALISON: Before "Bidlowitz" became "Biddle".

GENE: Well, if she knows her own history, which I seriously doubt, she would know that Jews— lapsed and otherwise—made up a full half of the volunteers that summer.

ALISON: Don't tell me. I was there—listening to you sing "This Little Light of Mine."

GENE: We were shoulder to shoulder with bull's-eyes on our backs. Two of our own already missing in Mississippi. And still we kept coming. Our Jewish professors filled us with dreams of capital J justice. Our Jewish lawyers faced down those red neck judges and kept us out of jail so we could march again. And what was the thanks we got? Stokely Carmichael threw us out of S N C C. Chanted "black power" with the Panthers and condemned Israel as a "racist state". Stokely Carmichael who grew up in the South Bronx with Jews. Best friend. Girlfriend. Stand-up guys who watched his back in the Irish and Italian neighborhoods. All of them Jews. And when have they ever watched our backs? Stood with us? Except to stand aside when Farrakhan called us devils? Well, I don't know about you, but I'm done being a political masochist.

ALISON: *(Pauses, then applauds)* What do you get for a speech like that these days? Twenty five, fifty grand?

GENE: There's no talking to you. There never was.

ALISON: You don't talk to people, you talk at them. You're still in love with the sound of your own voice.

GENE: Oh, give me a fucking break.

ALISON: You expected a thank-you note "Job well done"? Well, the job is not done. The job is so fucking undone it makes me sick.

GENE: And what did you learn in Mississippi?

ALISON: That you can change things if you're willing to put yourself on the line. And you don't do it for a "thank you." You do it because you believe in it. Honest to God, I read the newspaper and I don't know why there aren't people out on the streets everyday.

GENE: Nine Eleven is why. You don't have to bring the war home. Your Islamofascist friends already did.

ALISON: My friends? My real friends are inside these four walls.

GENE: Finally overcame that "white skin privilege," did you? And if you walk out of here next week do you really believe you'll ring up your guard friend, "Meet me at Starbucks, the first double latte is on me."

ALISON: I don't know Starbucks. I don't know double lattes. I've been in prison, you arrogant, malicious prick!

GENE: That's the Alison I remember. Come out swinging, lead with the chin. Boxer and brawler, classic match-up. *(Beat)* So I guess the small talk is over.

ALISON: You never could take a punch. Look what I've taken!

GENE: Martyrdom ill-suits you. It's pathologically narcissistic. You think a bomb went off and time stood still. We were about non-violent change. In a heartbeat, everything we stood for went up in smoke.

ALISON: I went to the hospital in handcuffs. You went to Scotland. Fucking Scotland. Go to Bangladesh, Somalia. Work on hunger, on drought. What's there to work on in Scotland—golf?

GENE: I worked in a housing project with skinhead gangs. Real National Front "Clockwork Orange" stuff. No weapons like American gangs. This is their weapon! *(Mimes a vicious head butt)* This is their weapon! *(Kicks savagely at the floor)* And I couldn't do a damned thing to stop them.

ALISON: You were a fair-weather conscientious objector.

GENE: Look, I didn't choose Scotland. Your father did.

ALISON: My father?

GENE: He didn't want the D A to subpoena me as a witness.

ALISON: And Arthur knew about this?

GENE: He bought me the ticket.

ALISON: No, you don't get off the hook that easy. Nobody made you go. You went.

GENE: I went because what happened at Grand Central was unconscionable.

ALISON: I know, I know. I *know*! And you were?...

GENE: Not there.

ALISON: Yeah, that's what you're good at. Being somewhere else! I was close enough to see the look in Officer Renshaw's eyes. *(Paces)* I'm just one of those "there" people. A woman here was dying of AIDS. Angela. She wanted me to be with her at the end. Just as she was taking her last breath, she saw me, and the bars. And the look in her eyes said, *I don't want to die here.* *(Beat)* Thirty years, Gene. You don't know what it's like. Your hair turns gray. Your insides dry up. You see yourself dying by inches.
   I...I don't, I don't want to die here...

GENE: Maybe you don't have to.

ALISON: I arranged a meeting with the daughter. That was a great idea. I don't know what else to do.

GENE: Let me help you.

ALISON: All we do is fight. Did we always?

GENE: Always. Because we're so much alike.

ALISON: We're nothing alike.

GENE: But we were good together.

ALISON: Name one time.

GENE: That last night.

ALISON: In the safe house?

GENE: Curled up together. Eating cookies.

ALISON: I couldn't sleep. We talked. You had all the answers. You always did.

GENE: But I was never the person you were.

ALISON: I don't even know what that means.

GENE: You said it yourself—with me there's no "there" there. Hell, I know I'm full of shit. I always talked a good game. I don't know, maybe I've built up this wall of words so I don't have to think of you rotting in this place. *(Beat)* But I do. I think about you all the time. I want to get you out of here. I want you to be free.

(They stare at each other. The stare becomes a lingering kiss that surprises both of them.)

ALISON: I want to trust you.

GENE: I'm tired of the whole game, Al.

ALISON: Exhaustion is not a basis for trust.

GENE: You're tired. Your guilt weighing you down.

ALISON: We all have our guilty secrets, don't we?

GENE: But we're not all coming up for parole. Give me something to take to the Parole Board. You could tell them what they want to hear. I could, for you. Not everything, just enough.

ALISON: What would I tell them?

GENE: Tell them just enough to turn the key, assuming you haven't already told them everything.

ALISON: I never said a word to anybody!

GENE: Not your father? Nor Arthur?

ALISON: Anybody. Ever.

GENE: *(Relieved)* Well, then we have something to talk about. I can offer you a chance to put things right.

ALISON: How?

GENE: Put it all on Malcolm.

ALISON: You're not asking me to name names, are you?

GENE: Malcolm's dead. Be smart for once. Tell them
he suckered you into his little death trip. Tell them you
were duped.

ALISON: That's very Roy Cohn of you.

GENE: I'm only asking for one name.

ALISON: You're asking me to renounce the movement.

GENE: I'm offering to write a letter to the Parole Board
and "C C" the White House.

ALISON: So you can parade me as your great political
rehab project?

ALISON: So we can finally put the past behind us.

ALISON: Just a neat little swap, huh?

GENE: What have you got to lose?

ALISON: My soul.

GENE: Get over yourself. This isn't a game. There aren't
any Get Out of Jail Free cards.

ALISON: One name is letting me off pretty easy.
What are we really talking here—a column, a radio
rant, a cable news show? What's my price tag, Gene?
What's the bottom line?

GENE: A book.

ALISON: Nobody gives a shit about me. I'm ancient
history.

GENE: You're a headline waiting to happen. Like it or
not, you're the poster girl for the failure of the Left.

ALISON: Fuck you. You don't have my permission to
write a book.

GENE: I don't need your permission.

ALISON: You approached Arthur with this "deal" at my father's funeral?

GENE: Arthur approached me. He came to me.

ALISON: Maybe I'll do some writing of my own.

GENE: Don't threaten me!

ALISON: I can do a lot more than that. I demand to speak to my attorney. I demand to speak to my attorney.

(UNEEQ *enters with* ARTHUR)

ALISON: I demand to speak to my attorney.

UNEEQ: Would you like me to terminate this visitation?

ALISON: I would like some straight answers from my attorney.

(UNEEQ *exits*)

ALISON: Why is he here, Arthur?

ARTHUR: He wanted to see you.

ALISON: We're miles past that pretext. He wants to write a book about me.

ARTHUR: *(To* GENE*)* You won't write a single page.

GENE: You think you can stop me?

ARTHUR: I have Howard's files. I know Malcolm asked you to help plant the bomb.

GENE: I said "no".

ARTHUR: And then you volunteered Alison.

ALISON: You volunteered me?

GENE: There was a collective discussion.

ALISON: When were you not the loudest voice in the room? That last night—you didn't have the balls to tell me?

GENE: You said "yes". That was your decision.

ARTHUR: I know Alison purchased the nails.

GENE: You don't know shit.

ARTHUR: And you were with her.

GENE: (To ALISON) You sell out like everyone else!

ALISON: I never told a living soul.

GENE: (Realizes ARTHUR has tricked him) You think you're pretty clever, don't you? Well fuck you and your lawyer tricks. Your partner was my attorney. You breach privilege and I'll have you disbarred.

ARTHUR: You're right. Any statement from me would be inadmissible. I can't say a word. But Alison can.

GENE: How can she tell the truth about me when she's never even told the truth about herself?

ALISON: I might, if it means bringing you down.

GENE: Who will take the word of a convicted felon? A murderer?

ALISON: I'm a human being.

GENE: You're not even alive. The movement died. And you died with it. Only nobody told you.

ALISON: Why do you hate me?

GENE: Because you hate this country!

ALISON: I squandered a human life, and it cost me my freedom. I wait in exile and pay and pay for my mistake while you run around cashing in on your little political freak show, all for the love of a buck. And that makes you a patriot?

GENE: I love this country.

ALISON: Well, if I ever get back to America, it will be with an immigrant's heart, my grandfathers heart. That's a love you'll never know. I pity you for calling it hate.

GENE: It didn't have to be this way, Al. It's not personal. It's politics.

(GENE *is suddenly isolated in light. He speaks deliberately—a man giving testimony.*)

GENE: Alison Moulton was an anarchist who wanted to overthrow our government with no better alternative in mind. That's because there is no better alternative to democracy. I recently spent time with her in prison, and I want to report that she is a changed woman, that she has seen the error of her ways. I want to, but I can't. Alison Moulton will never come before you to testify, because she fears the truth. Because she is still too filled with seditious rhetoric and slogan to confess to the murderous consequences of her ideological inadequacies and lies. Would she present a physical danger to society were she released? Certainly not. But her unrepentant self-righteousness means that she has not yet fully come to grips with the death of Officer Renshaw. And her release would constitute a far greater symbolic danger to our very way of life, which is currently under fanatical attack. Alison Moulton, I'm sad to say, is a terrorist. That is the verdict of history. And if there is any justice, it must also be the verdict of this Board.

(*Black out*)

Scene Five

(A prison conference room. ALISON *sits and addresses the unseen Parole Board.)*

ALISON: I want to thank the Parole Board for allowing me to make this last minute personal statement. Thirty... *(Coughs, clears her throat)* Thirty years ago, I set out from a tenement safe house on Avenue C. I had a grocery list: milk, eggs, butter, raisins, oatmeal. I had this idea I would make oatmeal cookies for a friend I was visiting. Why oatmeal cookies? It was kind of a running joke, because he was a Quaker. Oh, walnuts. Walnuts were also on the list, because that's how he liked his cookies.

I walked to the bodega on Avenue D. When I was checking out, the man behind the counter asked if there was anything else? I remembered something that wasn't on my list. An added ingredient that was on someone else's list. The words were out of my mouth before I knew what I was saying. "Do you have any nails?" "I've got some galvanized six penny roofers. Will that do the job?" "That'll do."

Back at the tenement, the oven is preheating to three-fifty. "Blind Faith" is on the turntable. I love baking to "Sea of Joy," and I can tell it's going to be a good batch because the album doesn't skip during the violin solo like it usually does. My friend, the Friend, shouts from the next room, "Don't forget the walnuts." I won't. I want this to be a perfect batch. Because tomorrow afternoon, I tell myself, I will walk into the Manhattan South Precinct and tell them my name is not Sondra Elliott, like it says on my driver's license and social security card. I will tell them my name is Alison Moulton and that I have an outstanding warrant for destruction of federal property in Chicago. I will tell

them that I have been living underground, and that
it is all behind me. Over. I am ready to accept the
consequences for what I have done. I am surfacing.
  I think all this knowing that at the exact same moment
in the basement of our tenement, a man is completing a
recipe of his own. I can picture every detail, as if I were
right there at his side. He carefully tapes dynamite to
a container. He attaches a timing device. He takes care
to wipe the surfaces with Vaseline so there is no static
electricity to arc the contacts and blow him to bits.
He reaches for the detonator, then pauses. There is
one more thing, a new ingredient. He reaches for the
brown paper bag and pours out galvanized six penny
nails. The recipe is complete.
  That night I can't sleep because of a picture in my
head. It is a poster we have been plastering on walls
and kiosks from coast to coast. It shows the results
of a five hundred pound cluster bomb on a village in
Cambodia.
A country that is not even "at war". The bomb would
have been a CBU 26, with six hundred and seventy
tennis ball-sized bomblets that break into two hundred
thousand steel fragments over hundreds of yards.
The pressure wave alone can burst your spleen.
A large piece of shrapnel will cut you in half. And
in this picture is a woman—the torso of a woman.
Her right arm is missing blow the elbow and I want to
think of her as Venus, the Cambodian goddess of love.
I love her, just as I love the soldiers who are suffering
needlessly in the jungles of Vietnam. But there are these
hateful objects scattered around her body. Dozens of
unexploded bomblets that will detonate when the goat
comes back to graze. When the woman's daughter
comes back to see what was once her mother. And the
poster is a failure. It reaches no one. Does not make this
anti-personnel—this inhuman!—device real. And so,
out of love for this woman, for mankind, we bring the

war home.

That night there's another picture in my head. A young woman in a pink villager blouse, a pleated skirt a discreet inch below the knee, shoulder length hair pulled back in a head band. You might think she's going on a first date. She is going to register voters in a rural Mississippi town where the local Klan has firebombed black churches and homes and beaten organizers bloody. She sets off down the road, and you know whatever lies ahead will change her life forever.

For me, that road sadly led to prison. Yet, everything I ever hoped to find in the outside world I have found it here. I have not been unaware of life beyond these borders. The global village extends even to inmates. I have been distant witness to the mounting terrors of the world. Religious fanaticism, imperial war, environmental suicide. As much as I crave life outside, it also terrifies me.

But the world should not be terrified of me. It was never my aim to hurt people. All I ever wanted to do in life is help. Yes, I am guilty. Guilty for not turning myself in sooner. Guilty for not warning Officer Renshaw. Guilty for providing the fatal ingredient. Guilty for taking a human life. Guilty for having too much "consciousness." There is not a day goes by that I am not conscious of the life I cut short and the pain I have caused his daughter. I stand here before you and accept responsibility for the thing I did. But I did not act alone! When I went to purchase those nails, at my side was...at my side...was every hope, every dream I ever had for America. Not the America that exploits fear, that profits from human misery. But the America that works for everything that is human, the America that is humane. I think I might yet resume that work. It would not erase the crime I committed. I can never hope for such grace. But I might find grace for others, with your

permission, in the name of the life I helped take.
  Thank you for your time.

Scene Six

(The prison library. ALISON *waits with* UNEEQ.*)*

UNEEQ: I heard about your statement.

ALISON: It was all wrong, wasn't it?

UNEEQ: It was an admission of guilt. Wrongdoing and accountability.

ALISON: *Crime and Punishment.*

UNEEQ: There were no "ifs" in it. You spoke from the heart. Anybody could see that.

ALISON: I made them uncomfortable.

UNEEQ: Nobody said that.

ALISON: They looked away a lot. Fidgeted. I'm fucked.

UNEEQ: Don't jump to conclusions. I used to jump to conclusions all the time.

ALISON: Like?

UNEEQ: You. First time we met I jumped to the conclusion that you were some spoiled rich bitch who got what was coming to you.

ALISON: I make a better second impression?

UNEEQ: Not really. But once I got to know you, I didn't mind you so much. As far as what you're in here for, well, I don't make judgments. That's for people who got to make themselves feel superior.

ALISON: You don't need to feel superior to me?

UNEEQ: Naw. Thought I'd let you feel equal.

ALISON: Thank you.

UNEEQ: You weren't one hundred percent honest to that Board, though, were you?

ALISON: I don't know how to do honesty in percents.

UNEEQ: You could've given them a name so they'd go easier on you.

ALISON: I took a solemn oath never to reveal the names of people in the movement.

UNEEQ: Even when they shootin" their mouth off and fuckin" you up the ass with the Parole Board?

ALISON: Even then.

UNEEQ: I'm just saying you maybe could've escaped this place.

ALISON: Maybe. But I can't escape from myself.

(The buzzer sounds and ARTHUR *enters holding an envelope. He hands it to* ALISON.)

ARTHUR: Here it is.

ALISON: I can't. You...

*(*ALISON *hands the envelope to* ARTHUR.)

ARTHUR: "State of New York Division of Parole. After a full review of the record and interview, the Panel has determined that given the violent nature of your offense and the credible argument that your release might be construed by some to diminish respect for the law, to nonetheless grant your request for parole, consistent with pre-release screening procedures. The reasons for approval are listed below."

Blah-blah-blah. "...including a written statement of support from Officer Uneeq Edmonds."

ALISON: Muz Edmonds!

UNEEQ: It wasn't anything.

ALISON: What did you say?

UNEEQ: I told them about how Jesus raised up Lazarus from the dead and gave him a second chance at life. I told them they won't find that in the Hebrew bible. But I found it in the Hebrew heart. I've seen with my own eyes what you do for people. Not because you expect something back. Just because doing is what you do to be human. I told them I know you helped take Officer Renshaw's life. But now you've taken him into your heart. There's none of us can raise that man out of his grave. But we can give him a second chance by giving you a second chance. I wasn't asking for any miracles from that Parole Board. I was just asking them to be human. These days that's miracle enough. *(Beat)* I don't want no "thank you"s, alright?

ALISON: Maybe we can get together once I'm out.

UNEEQ: You think so?

ALISON: Coffee or something.

UNEEQ: I'm partial to double lattes. *(Exits)*

ALISON: I wish Howard had lived to see this day.

ARTHUR: He would have been very proud of you. I'm very proud of you.

ALISON: Arthur, I did a terrible thing. *(Breaks down)*

ARTHUR: I know. I know.

ALISON: I'm scared. I don't know what's out there. I feel like I did all those years ago when I got on the bus to Mississippi.

ARTHUR: That took some balls.

ALISON: We had bail money, medical contact numbers, and a list of instructions: don't stand in an open lit doorway; don't look white citizens in the eye; if you're beaten, roll up in a ball and protect your head. *(Beat)* It

would have been so easy to stay home. Do nothing.
I wasn't even old enough to vote. Why did I go? I kept
asking myself. Then I found this in Howard's sweater.
(Unfolds the paper she found) It's a flyer. I gave it to him
before I got on the bus. *(Shows him the paper)* "Come Let
Us Build a New World Together." Does that make any
sense?

ARTHUR: No sense at all. *(He exits.)*

*(*ALISON *slowly crosses upstage, turns away, then turns
back.)*

(Blackout)

END OF PLAY